FAITH BYTES

Faith Bytes

Listening to the Heart of God

Sunday Reflections - Year A

RICHARD LEONARD, SJ

Paulist Press
New York / Mahwah, NJ

Cover image by agsandrew/Shutterstock.com
Cover and book design by Lynn Else

Library of Congress Cataloging-in-Publication Data available upon request.

ISBN 978-0-8091-4970-4 (paperback)
ISBN 978-0-8091-8978-6 (ebook)

Published by Paulist Press
997 Macarthur Boulevard
Mahwah, NJ 07430
www.paulistpress.com

Printed and bound in the
United States of America

Dedication

My newest grandnephew, Leonard, Elisabeth, James & Patrick, Meg, Therese & Paul, Mary Louise, Anna & Grant, Lee & Athol, Mark & Fiona, Mary RSCJ, Nancy & Tony, Ignatius & Tracey, Angela & Ben whose goodness and support enlivens my faith

Contents

Acknowledgments

Paul McMahon, Bob Byrns, and the team at Paulist Press for their continuing belief in my work, and for enabling me to talk to a very wide audience about faith and culture;

Vu Kim Quyen, SJ, and the Australian Province of the Society of Jesus for the education and formation I have received and their ongoing support to do the "greatest good for the greatest number";

The Jesuit community and parish of North Sydney/Kirribilli/Lavender Bay, Australia, without whom these reflections would never have emerged. They who help me taste and see that the Lord is good, and sometimes stand with me when faith bites.

Introduction

As the current pastor of a busy and active Jesuit parish in Sydney, Australia: Our Lady of the Way, North Sydney/Lavender Bay/Kirribilli, we completed a parish census last year, for the first time in many years. Deepening our identity as a synodal church, we consulted the whole community about their priorities as a Catholic parish. By an overwhelming margin, the top priority was attracting young adults to the parish and keeping them. In fact, for ninety-five percent of all respondents, this was their primary issue.

In response to that feedback, I met with our Gen Zers about how we might achieve this goal of reaching out to young adults. We already have a very engaging young adult liturgy on Sunday night. My young parishioners told me that "for our peers to come back to Mass, they need to know that we are a welcoming and hospitable community, that we practice what we preach in our outreach to poor and those on the margins, that we offer good music and liturgy, and that the preaching gives a relevant message for the week ahead."

To that end, we started a YouTube channel where the young adults posted the full versions of my weekly homilies. From these sermons they edited down bite-sized grabs for Facebook and Instagram. It has taken off modestly and has indeed attracted some young people to join us regularly. I don't know another Sydney parish that would have as many young adults attending Sunday Mass as we do.

This book has emerged out of this process. Here are 62 short, direct, and meaningful reflections for Year A, the Year of Matthew. Over the next year, we will explore the major themes of Matthew's Gospel: Jesus as the fulfillment of Old Testament prophecy; the "Kingdom of Heaven" as the central focus of Jesus's teaching; Jesus as the New Moses; the demands of discipleship within the community of believers, the Church; the conflicts with religious authorities and the challenge to practice what we believe; the end of time and the judgement of the "Son of Man"; and how mercy, justice, and righteousness do not come from external observances, but from a heart converted to Jesus Christ.

I acknowledge the great work done by Daniel J. Harrington, SJ, in "The Gospel of Matthew," in the first volume of the Sacra Pagina series, (Liturgical Press, 2007), and Brendan Byrne, SJ, in *Lifting the Burden: Reading Matthew's Gospel in the Church Today* (Liturgical Press, 2004).

I didn't come up with the title Faith Bytes, but I like it very much, playing as it does with the term that is synonymous with the new technologies. These platforms, at their best, are the marketplace within which we must now proclaim the Gospel. And especially in Matthew, we see that our faith in Jesus often bites into our complacency, calling us to truth, sacrifice, justice, humility, and radical love.

ADVENT

1

In the Light

Isaiah 2:1–5; Romans 13:11–14;
Matthew 24:37–44

Being in the light is not just about what we see; it is about what we do.

St. Ignatius encourages us to be alert to all the ways we con ourselves that keeping secrets hidden in the dark is a necessary or acceptable way to live. He was a great fan of preparation. He was convinced that the best spirituality was one that kept reflecting on daily existence to see the pattern of God's goodness drawing us into the light, and the sometimes-unexpected moments in the day when we are plunged into darkness.

The season of Advent is the time when we remember what it was like to wait and hope and long for the Messiah to come. It parallels all those moments in our lives when we wait for Christ to break in upon our day with gifts of saving love. In this season may we bring to consciousness and to God all the things that stop us from being fully alive and bask in the freedom and light Christ wants us to have.

2

Comforting the Afflicted

Isaiah 11:1–10; Romans 15:4–9;
Matthew 3:1–12

In Christianity, there is an important distinction between personal and private faith. Personal faith knows that God is close and intimate, which is what we celebrate at Christmas. We should always be careful of hymns that only speak about "me and Jesus against the world." Inheriting the promises made to Israel and seeing them as intended for all God's children, we believe we are saved as a people. For us, it is "we and Jesus for the world."

If we have no interest in justice, development, and peace for our world, if we don't care to know our fellow parishioners or if all we want is to be left alone to come to Mass, say our prayers, and save our souls, then we need to hear the story of Christmas all over again.

May this Advent, then, see John the Baptist do what he does best: comfort the afflicted and afflict the comfortable.

3

A Vital Message

Isaiah 35:1–6a, 10; James 5:7–10;
Matthew 11:2–11

The first reading and the Gospel make it very clear that farmers never put down tools just because the rain comes. We're told that because we are soaked in the love of God, we are called to do all we can for those in our world who are lame, blind, deaf, lepers, poor, and anyone left for dead.

This is a vital message for us to hear today because there are some who tell us that all we have to do is look after "our own backyard." Advent reminds us that by welcoming Christ we have an obligation to care for all children. Everywhere is our backyard because that's where our brothers and sisters live. May we gain from Christ the generosity to see that the desert is meant to bloom for all people, not just a few of us lucky to live in an oasis.

Our goodness remains a most powerful sign of God's salvation that is seen more so in deeds than in words.

4

God-with-Us

Isaiah 7:10–14; Romans 1:1–7;
Matthew 1:18–24

As I gathered with my family in front of an overblown meal which none of us could finish, holding expensive gifts we didn't need and drinking more alcohol than was necessary, I thought, "We've lost the plot with Christmas." God-with-us arrives as a simple child in need of love; and in the honor of that day we spend money, eat too much, and get drunk.

I left the table, went to my desk, and wrote a card for each member of my family. I told them what I'd never been able to say: "I want you to know I love you."

When they read those cards, my family thought I was losing it, but God visited me in the last week of Advent, and Christmas will never be the same again.

CHRISTMAS

5

Be Not Afraid

Isaiah 9:1–6; Titus 2:11–14; Luke 2:1–14

St. Paul tells us that love drives out all fear. That's who we celebrate this Christmas: love taken human form in Jesus Christ the Lord. Thus today we remember the birthday of a man whose life, death, and resurrection showed us the way out of our fears, revealed the truth that sets us free, and gave us the life that we can live to the full in this world, and in the next.

Christmas is the feast when God calls us to be as active as we can in bringing Christ's kingdom to bear in our world.

Christmas is the feast when our memories are joined to God's, who has remembered us in our fear.

Christmas is the feast when all Christian relationships are defined by the dignity, trust, and respect they bestow on us and on those we relate to.

As a result of the babe of Bethlehem, God has shown us that fear is not our calling, and that the saving love of Jesus impels us to take risks in how we live out our faith, hope, and love.

On any day, then, in the coming year, when we face down our fears and live our Christian life to the full, we'll discover that Christmas is a moveable feast.

6

Holiness

Sirach 3:3–7, 14–17a; Colossians 3:12–21; Matthew 2:13–15, 19–23

The feast of the Holy Family tells us that Jesus, Mary, and Joseph had a career in holiness.

The problem with holiness is that we often equate it with perfection. To be a holy person does not mean one is perfect. Perfection rests only in God. Jesus enjoyed perfection in his humanity, but we must allow Mary and Joseph to be less than perfect, or else we make them truly divine as well. As a family, they were not perfect, they were holy. They struggled together to understand the best way they could bring God's reign to bear in our world. Their destinies were vastly different but intimately connected. They needed each other.

If we allow the Holy Family to be too removed from our experience, they have little to say about the fights, misunderstandings, and problems that can sometimes characterize our families. If on the other hand, we concede that Jesus, Mary, and Joseph, as a family, were not perfect, they can be a model of the very thing we want in our own homes: a love, justice, fidelity, and kindness that reveal a life of holiness. They can show us a mutual respect that allows each family member to find his or her own path to revealing God's creative and saving love for our world. And they can provide us with the assurance of knowing that, because of their holiness, we have all been welcomed into the family of God.

7

Wonder or Fear

Isaiah 60:1–6; Ephesians 3:2–3a, 5–6; Matthew 2:1–12

So often our reactions to Jesus can be like Herod's. We can be threatened and frightened. We want to eliminate the voices that call us to live out the reign of God, and that remind us of the costs involved. Matthew tells us that the enemy of the Christian life is fear. It entraps us and infects those around us. And we are often most fearful when we risk losing power, so we lie, are deceitful, and cheat to maintain our position at all costs.

But when we face down our fears and name the real threats in our life, we know the overwhelming joy of finding the "Morning Star who came back from the dead and shed his peaceful light on all humanity."

So, this story is far more than a travelogue of exotic Persian kings. It's the story of the choices that lie before all Christians everywhere: Do we want to live out of wonder or fear?

To follow Jesus' rule is to keep our eyes on that Star that lights the path to having the courage to live out his gospel, to carry our crosses, whatever they be, and to trust that God will remain faithful to *us* through death, into eternal life—where threats and fears will be no more.

To the degree that we live beyond our fears right here and now, we enjoy our very own Epiphany, wonder-filled as it is!

8

The Greatness of God's Love

Isaiah 42:1–4, 6–7; Acts 10:34–38; Matthew 3:13–17

When we are baptized in Christ, we acknowledge both original sin and original grace. God's love comes alive in us even though we are aware of how far from that love we stray.

The baptism of Jesus, and every baptism done in his name ever since, is the moment when we hold together the greatness of God's love, which calls each of us by name to be his son or daughter, with the reality of our human frailty. What more appropriate way of welcoming anyone into the world than having a community of frail, human believers initiate its members by reminding them that original sin does not have the last word. For those of us baptized in Christ, the Father's love always and everywhere has the final, appropriate say on every matter.

May this feast make us worthy of the love lavished on us in our baptisms and give us the courage to keep doing the appropriate things for the coming generations.

ORDINARY TIME—I

9

The Suffering Servant

Isaiah 49:3, 5–6; 1 Corinthians 1:1–3; John 1:29–34

Saying Jesus is the Lamb of God is a shorthand way of telling us two things. The first is that Jesus is God's most precious gift: God's own self, given to the world that we might know how serious God is about us. God can give us nothing more than Jesus. As a result of Jesus's innocent suffering and death there is no need for any lambs to be religiously slaughtered ever again.

We need to keep hearing this message because some Christians get caught into glorifying Jesus' suffering so much, they get trapped in their own world of pain and go looking for more. Jesus never sought out suffering. He bore what came his way. Most of us don't need to look for more suffering in our lives because we share in the Lamb of God's sacrifice in the ordinary down times of our own lives.

Secondly, John knew that *talya*, the Aramaic word for sheep, is the same word used for "servant." Jesus is the servant who brings us the truth we need for life, who answers our deepest desires to know that our existence has meaning and purpose, and he opens for us the life beyond this one, where there will be no more weeping or sadness.

Jesus shows us that when we are baptized into his death and enter his service we also share in his resurrection and glory because he bears, and bears away, the sins of the world.

10

Unity

Isaiah 8:23b—9:3;
1 Corinthians 1:10–13, 17; Matthew 4:12–23

The church has a wonderful diversity, a plurality of expression, emphasis, and culture. It's always been like this. It means the church is taking seriously its role of finding Christ in every place and every community in the world. The moment we pit one local church against the other ("I prefer the pope to my bishop") we lose the Catholic communion in Christ Jesus that holds us together.

Paul tells us that preaching the cross of Jesus is the mission of the church. Jesus shows us in the Gospel that teaching, preaching, and healing are the hallmarks of his ministry. And the same should hold for us....

To the degree to which we live this out in our communion with our local successor to the apostles, the more chance all members of the church have to use the energy and gifts given at baptism to do what Christ wants of the church: to change the world for good and be a beacon of Christ's saving gifts—faith, hope, and charity.

11

Jesus as Friend

Zephaniah 2:3; 3:12–13;
1 Corinthians 1:26–31; Matthew 5:1–12a

The Sermon on the Mount is one of the greatest sermons ever given. What makes it great is not just the beauty of its language or the hope of its theology. It is truly great because Jesus was preaching to the reality in front of him....When Jesus says, "Blessed are you," he is not being patronizing, glossing over all sorts of tough human realities.

In the Hebrew scriptures, a blessing is the discovery that God is present and active in one's experience, right here and right now. So, the Beatitudes are saying that you do not need to go past your own daily struggles to find the presence of God. Jesus tells us that if we are poor, compassionate, mournful, campaigning for a just society and suffering because of it, gentle, innocent, a peacemaker or a martyr, we are encountering, in a special way, the presence of God.

Jesus is the best friend we could ever have, interested in every daily event, and he's there for us at every moment in life. Yet he doesn't barge in. He waits patiently for an invitation to enter our lives at whatever level we want. He meets us where we are, embraces us, holds us close when the going gets tough, and helps us find the way forward. Jesus-as-friend is the greatest Beatitude of all.

12

Faith

Isaiah 58:7–10; 1 Corinthians 2:1–5;
Matthew 5:13–16

We are told that, if salt has lost its taste, it's good for nothing. So, the challenge is to keep it fresh so it can keep doing its job. Jesus suggests that, in the same way, we must be on guard to make sure that our faith remains fresh so it's able to do its job as well.

Jesus tells us that a hollow attachment to the letter of the law, unbridled anger, an inability to forgive, being unfaithful in marriage, seeking revenge on our enemies, not being true to our word, and being enslaved by money are all examples of bad faith.

More positively, Jesus tells us that prayer, being generous to the poor, being discerning about whom we spend time with, what we see and hear, and going without things we often consider essential are helpful to living a faith-filled life.

The job of faith is to enable us to live out and build Christ's reign of justice and love in this world as a foretaste of what awaits us in heaven.

13

Eyes on Christ

Sirach 15:16–21; 1 Corinthians 2:6–10;
Matthew 5:17–37

The greatest aid to living this challenging life is Christ. He is the letter, the stroke of the letter, and the accomplishment of the law. Having a transparent relationship with Christ, and the community who follows his way, enables us to fulfill the greatest law of all: the law of love, from which all other laws are judged.

So, with our eyes on Christ, and supporting, enabling, and challenging each other, we go from here as followers of Jesus, at home and in society, known by name and nature to be forgiving, reconciling, faithful, discerning, true to our word, shunning the courts, and giving dignity and respect to everyone we meet.

14

Forgiveness

Leviticus 19:1–2, 17–18; 1 Corinthians 3:16–23; Matthew 5:38–48

In the Gospel, Jesus quotes Exodus 21:23–24: that the law required there be a "life for life, eye for eye, tooth for tooth, hand for hand, foot for foot." It is also repeated in the books of Leviticus and Deuteronomy. It has come to be called the Law of Retribution. And as barbaric as this law sounds to us today, in its time it was a moderating influence in society.

Jesus inherits and understands this tradition, but clearly makes a break with it, and that's where we stand.

This is a tough Gospel, maybe as tough as it gets, because it asks us to go against the most seductive part of our human nature: getting even. It applies to the relative we won't speak to, the former spouse against whom we poison our children, the neighbor we delight in annoying, and the work colleague we bad-mouth because he or she got the promotion we were after.

But Jesus's words equally apply to those who commit criminal acts against us or others, and the enemies of our state. This is why the church takes a stand against the death penalty and unjust wars. The amazing thing is that revenge and retribution solves nothing. It just eats us up and usually continues the conflict, inflames the anger, and distorts us into something much less than God intended.

Let's pray then for the Holy Spirit to help us conquer our pride, so that we can live more peacefully with ourselves, and see how the gift of forgiveness is much more caught than taught.

15

Pride and Greed

Isaiah 49:14–15; 1 Corinthians 4:1–5;
Matthew 6:24–34

God and wealth can get in the way of one another. The problem is not being wealthy. The issue is what wealth does to us, how it changes us and can distort our priorities. In the Catholic tradition we have a name for the two obstacles that seduce us away from a godly use of wealth. They're two of the seven deadly sins: pride and greed....

It would be a mistake to hear Jesus's words this week as only applying to our personal wealth. It does that all right, but in a world where economics and business faculties are the fastest growing schools on campus, where "mom and dad stockholders," mostly through ignorance, sacrifice conscience for profits, and where, in our nation and in the world, the rich are getting richer while the poor are dying, the social gospel also asks us what sort of ethical business culture we want.

We can keep saying that we want to smell the flowers and live a simple life. If we are serious about it, we better start working on the pride and greed that can corrupt us personally, corporately, and as a nation. For what will it profit us to gain the entire world, and lose our very souls?

LENT & HOLY WEEK

16

Letting God In

Joel 2:12–18; 2 Corinthians 5:20—6:2; Matthew 6:1–6, 16–18

The Christian tradition has not tended to make much of a distinction between privacy and secrecy. But they are very different realities and exercise diverse powers in our lives. Privacy is something we are all entitled to, both in the personal and social sphere. Privacy protects our rights and dignity.

Secrecy is where information is concealed out of fear of detection. Think for a moment of the number of families who have a secret that can never be spoken. Secrets are not about confidentiality; they are about control.

In Lent this year, we could do no better than privately and quietly reviewing our life and seeing where the bad spirit has us in its grip. What parts of our life do we work hard to cover up? These are the hiding places where the Divine Physician wants to make a house call. God knows where to go; all we have do is let God in.

17

Knowledge

Genesis 2:7–9; 3:1–7; Romans 5:12–19; Matthew 4:1–11

The Genesis story about the origins of sin in the world rewards very careful reading. The serpent promises Eve two things: that her eyes will be opened to know good from evil and that this will make her like God. Such a temptation was irresistible, and nothing has changed.

Knowledge is a gift given to us by God. As anxious as the church has sometimes been about scientific investigations, our best traditions see God revealed in human thoughts and scientific achievements that ennoble our human family. It is the application of knowledge, or the way it is abused, that is harmful.

This week's Gospel is about knowledge too. Satan knows who Jesus is. His temptations are an attempt to get Jesus to betray his humanity and not endure the limitations of his daily life. Jesus knows that the only way to be true to his divinity is to allow us to see it shine in and through his human life. The rejection of the temptation to compromise his frail human frame gives us the hope that we, too, can glimpse the power of God's greatness in every moment we reject the desire to be directors of our own destiny and to see good triumph over evil in the choices we make.

It's a relief to know we don't have to be God! May this Lent see us do what we are created for: to use all our knowledge to praise, reverence, and serve the Loving One who willed us into being.

18

Penance

Genesis 12:1–4a; 2 Timothy 1:8b–10; Matthew 17:1–9

Just when some of us think Lent is a grim season of self-denial, the church gives us the story of Jesus's transfiguration to put our sacrifices in context. The only reason we deny ourselves anything or commit ourselves to actions of service for these forty days is to grow more deeply in love with the God who loves us into life.

Penance is not meant to attack our self-esteem; it's intended to help us sort out what really matters, to cast some light in the darkness of our lives, and to focus on the relationship that gives meaning and purpose for this world and the next.

19

The Gift of Life

Exodus 17:3–7; Romans 5:1–2, 5–8;
John 4:5–42

At that famous well, Jesus enters the world of a poor Samaritan woman who has been dumped five times by the men who married her. By asking for a drink, by engaging her in conversation, by understanding her situation, and offering her a way out of the cycle of emotional abuse in which she was caught, Jesus gives her the greatest gift of all: personal dignity. This changes her life and turns her into one of the earliest missionaries in John's Gospel.

A drink of water helped a Samaritan woman confront the embarrassment of her world, their quick and inaccurate judgments, and reassess the choices that could lead them to life. No matter how good the gift of water was that day, the unknown and unexpected Giver of the gift was so much greater. May the season of Lent help us do the same.

20

Seeing

1 Samuel 16:1b, 6–7, 10–13a;
Ephesians 5:8–14;
John 9:1–41

On reflection, the Gospel of the man born blind is a joyful one. Imagine this man's elation at having his sight restored. As the story develops, the all-seeing Pharisees move to spiritual blindness by putting on the blinkers of the law. They cannot recognize Jesus or his works of mercy because of their tunnel vision. Jesus doesn't fit their worldview. Meanwhile, the blind beggar, who has sight restored, goes on to gain insight about who Jesus is and the way that God works in the world; he begins to see how shallow and pathetic the Pharisees really are.

Disability and illness do not come from personal sinfulness....It's true that God permits us to live in an imperfect world where we are prone to illness and disability. But that same world gives us the freedom to be creative in the face of adversity, to be compassionate with those who are sick or disabled, and to be free to believe that there is a purpose for each human life. God, the source of all life, does not actively send bad things to us, instead, he is our constant companion in dealing with them, giving us the courage and strength to cope with, and sometimes overcome, them.

May it never be said of us that we were so consumed by our own religious vision that we missed God's woods for the trees.

21

Come Forth!

Ezekiel 37:12–14; Romans 8:8–11;
John 11:1–45

The season of Lent has its origins in third-century Egypt, where there was a commemoration of Jesus' forty days in the desert. In the fourth century, these forty days were moved to their present location in the church's calendar as the final preparation time for baptismal candidates at Easter, and by the fifth century these penitential and baptismal focuses came together as one season for all believers to observe. Even the word *Lent,* from the old English word *lencten,* meaning spring, alerted Christians in the northern hemisphere that this season was linked to the waking of nature after the long sleep of winter. Lent is about waking up to see that light and life have come in Christ.

On this last Sunday in Lent, Lazarus is given to us to help us think about the tombs in which we lie hidden from the life to which we are called. But this Sunday, Jesus stands at the entrance of our tombs and calls us out of them. We're asked to face down the bad spirit that keeps us locked in secrecy, to move away from shame, embrace repentance, recognize the price to be paid for being true to what's best in ourselves, and we're invited to know the light and life of Christ's healing and forgiveness.

May the Eucharist allow us to see the Lord stand at our tomb and gently call us by name, "Come forth!" And at his word may we be unbound and let free.

22

Silence

Procession: Matthew 21:1–11;
Isaiah 50:4–7; Philippians 2:6–11;
Matthew 26:14—27:66

In our journey of faith, we should always be on guard against being part of a manipulated crowd. The unchecked enthusiasm of a crowd can carry us away to places, people, or things we would not ordinarily choose and should not embrace. We only need to look at the power of the media and advertising to see how susceptible we are to becoming a slave to fashionable ideologies, dress codes, and what and who is in or out.

The story of Passion Sunday is that manipulation of a crowd, even by legitimate authorities, can be the beginning of spiritual death.

So, what's the remedy to being manipulated, to regaining a sense of what really matters, and standing up against the crowd for the values we know are right? It starts with silence. It's being a contemplative in a manic world and praying for the courage to dissent from the crowd's hyped-up madness.

May we model our lives on Jesus in every way by creating the silence we need in our lives to sort out our priorities in a world that loves words.

23

The Breaking of the Bread

Exodus 12:1–8, 11–14;
1 Corinthians 11:23–26; John 13:1–15

Whatever else the Eucharist meant to the early church, the action of breaking apart and pouring out captured how they wanted to remember Jesus and the meal he gave them. To this day, the liturgy maintains a connection with this legacy in the *fractio panis,* the breaking of the bread, during which we sing the Lamb of God.

If Easter is to come alive for us, we must be prepared to be broken and poured out in love for our world....Every time we come forward and receive communion, we say "Amen" to Jesus Christ as body broken and blood poured out. In doing so, we reaffirm that this is how much God loves us. This is also the intimate moment where God meets us in the most broken parts of our lives and in the times that we feel completely poured out. God is a companion in our suffering and sacrifices. In turn, it shows us how we should live. Everyone who receives Christ in communion says they are prepared to pay the price of being one with him in being broken and poured out in love for the world.

By taking up Jesus's commission to serve, we show how his life, death, and resurrection continue to "Easter in us" and change the world for good. We are people who look for opportunities to take up the commission to serve all those who feel spent with the brokenness of their lives.

24

The Cross

Isaiah 52:13—53:12;
Hebrews 4:14–16; 5:7–9; John 18:1—19:42

The good news today is that apprehension, accusation, and denial were not the last words in Jesus's life. And because of him, they're not the last words in our lives either.

No matter what we've done or what we're doing, nothing can separate us from the love of God poured out in Jesus Christ the Lord. No matter what crosses we carried to Good Friday, we believe that God's commitment to us was such that he even went to suffering and death to reveal his saving love.

If we feel apprehensive, allow Christ to arrest us with his peace. If we stand accused of destructive behavior, allow Christ to convert our hearts and change our lives. If we deny Christ by what we say or how we live, let's decide today to be as faithful to him as he is to us.

By doing this, a surprising thing will happen. Even while carrying our own crosses, we will feel the weight lifted as the one who loves us helps shoulder our burdens as well.

No wonder we call this solemn feast "Good Friday." What greater goodness could we know than that the cross of Jesus reveals that our God, whether named or not, is our companion at every step of life's journey?

EASTER

25

New Life

Genesis 1:1—2:2; 22:1–18; Exodus 14:15—15:1; Isaiah 54:5–14; 55:1–11; Baruch 3:9–15, 32—4:4; Ezekiel 36:16–17a, 18–28; Romans 6:3–11; Matthew 28:1–10

As Christians, Easter joy is meant to mark our lives—though if some of us are truly joyful we should start by telling our faces about it! Not that we can, or should, walk around perpetually smiling. Christian joy is more profound than that. It's about facing up to the most difficult and tragic moments in our lives knowing that we don't have to be afraid, that God's faithful love will see life win out over death.

We all know this is easier said than done. Take the Gospel for example. The women are told twice to tell the disciples to go to Galilee where they will meet Jesus for themselves.

Galilee does not have to be a place for us. It's a situation, a frame of mind, or a choice we make. Our Galilee could be the desolate journey of physical, emotional, or spiritual pain. It could be dashed promises, broken relationships, or unrealized hopes. Whatever it is, this night promises us that Christ is not only there when we arrive, he has gone ahead of us, to that desolate place, so that we might have loving arms in which to fall at journey's end.

The reason we are so exultant is that the first Jerusalem did not have the last word in Jesus' life. God did. So, all our deaths in Jerusalem and all our fearful, anxious trips to Galilee can end in new life and fresh starts.

26

Called by Name

Acts 10:34a, 37–43;
Colossians 3:1–4 *or* 1 Corinthians 5:6b–8;
John 20:1–9 *or* Matthew 28:1–10;
Evening: Luke 24:13–35

The most important thing we know about Mary Magdalene is that she is the first to experience the Risen Christ and is the first Christian missionary, the apostle to the apostles. One detail is especially poignant in the week's Gospel. We're told that Mary encountered the Risen Christ while weeping outside Jesus's tomb. She felt a double loss on that first Easter Sunday. Not only was she grieving for the loss of the One whom she had seen tortured to death, but she also wept for what she thought was the ultimate insult inflicted on Him—the desecration of his grave and the stealing of his corpse.

Mary Magdalene is the patron saint of those of us who have ever stood at tombs and wept. And she shows us that amid any grief Christ comes to us and calls by name. Because of Mary's tears and even more because of her evangelization, we believe that there is not a human being who has died in the last year, or any year, who is not known to God by name. God makes no distinction between the rich or poor, whether we are from a developing or developed country, whether we are Christian, Muslim, or atheist; we are all called by name to share in his life according to the grace which has enabled us to do so. God knows not only our name; he knows our heart, our history, and our selves.

27

The Journey of Faith

Acts 2:42–47; 1 Peter 1:3–9;
John 20:19–31

The Gospel story about doubting Thomas has to be one of the most misunderstood episodes in the New Testament. If you're like me, for years we have been consoled by Thomas doubting that Jesus had been raised from the dead. Thomas's doubts were in Jesus, we have been led to believe. But let's read the story very carefully. It's not Jesus Thomas doubts, it's the disciples. In fact, when Jesus appears to them seven days later, Thomas has the opportunity to share in the experience of the Risen Lord and like the others he immediately confesses Easter faith.

There are three elements in this story that should give us great comfort. The first is that Thomas doubts the early church, and not just regarding a minor issue of discipline or procedure. He doubts the central Christian message: that God raised Jesus from the dead.

The second consoling fact concerns the earliest church. Even though they are filled with the presence of the Risen Lord and though Thomas refuses to believe their witness, they remain faithful to him in his doubts.

The final element concerns the significance of the time between the first and second appearances of Jesus. The creation of the early church, the movement of its earliest leaders from timidity to boldness, took time, and Christ is present at every step of the church's creation and re-creation. Our fidelity to one another on the long journey of faith is only surpassed by our crucified God who does not give up on us, no matter how many questions we ask or how much we doubt.

28

Christ Is Risen

Acts 2:14, 22–23; 1 Peter 1:17–21;
Luke 24:13–35

Every Sunday, as part of our journey of faith, we embark on our road to Emmaus. There is never any point in us coming here pretending to be different from how we actually feel and who we are. God sees our heart and mind and wants to meet us in the midst of our life, whatever it may be like. The Emmaus story teaches us that Jesus first wants to listen to us before he wants us to listen to him.

Emmaus, however, was not just about the disciples and their lives, in the same way that the Eucharist is not just about our lives either. Christ opens the scriptures to us each week so that we can make sense of our experience, see the ways in which God is present and absent, and recognize our own foolishness. As with the Emmaus disciples, we are welcomed to the table of the Lord where we recognize Christ in the breaking of the bread and the pouring of the cup. This meal enables us to go out from here and proclaim to all we meet that Christ is risen.

29

The Voice of Jesus

Acts 2:14a, 36–41;
1 Peter 2:20b–25; John 10:1–10

In our world there are a multitude of voices clamoring for attention. The loudest voices we hear are not always the wisest ones. Jesus invites us to attune our listening to the sound of his voice so that even if it is faintly heard amid the noise, we can lift our heads, turn our gaze, and walk toward it.

More than ever, there are some voices that entice us away from the gospel. We are told that it is impossible to be happy unless we are wealthy; impossible to be fulfilled unless we are sexually active with several partners; impossible to be free unless we answer to no one.

And in this crowded marketplace the voice of Jesus keeps saying the same thing it's been saying for two thousand years. Happiness is found in sharing what we can with the poor, in being faithful and loving in all our relationships, and in surrendering our freedom to the service of his kingdom of justice and peace.

30

The Way, the Truth, and the Life

Acts 6:1–7; 1 Peter 2:4–9; John 14:1–12

For many people, "going home" means a return to comfort and security.

It's not by accident that the image of Jesus preparing us a house and being the Way, the Truth, and the Life are put together in this week's Gospel. We are told to make a home in him as he makes a home in us. What a terrific image of the intimacy Christ wants to share with us, and we with him!

The best homes, however, do not just protect and keep their occupants safe for eternity. A home is a means to an end, which is to give us the stability and sanity we need to keep going out into the world beyond it. In the same way, our home of faith with Jesus enables us to keep going out to a sometimes-hostile world and share with others the Way, the Truth, and the Life that sustains us.

The Way we follow is about justice, development, and peace for all people everywhere and not just the select few who can build the biggest mansions on earth. We are invited to keep speaking the Truth even if that makes us unpopular or different or at odds with the majority. And we have to keep living the Life that sees that our greatest joy comes from human dignity being celebrated everywhere.

31

The Law of Love

Acts 8:5–8, 14–17; 1 Peter 3:15–18; John 14:15–21

There are two strong images in this week's Gospel: the law and love. This can seem curious to modern ears because we have been duped into thinking that the law is the enemy of love, and that only freedom and joy are love's fruits. But think for a moment of people or projects we love, ones to which we are committed. We don't need a rule book to call us to the most generous and sacrificial behavior in their regard. We respond "above and beyond the call of duty" not because of the law, but because of love. Jesus teaches us today that obedience to his commandments is a subset of our loving relationship with him.

The word *obedience* comes from the Latin word *oboedire,* meaning "to listen carefully." That's a gentler way of understanding Jesus' call. The more obedient we are to Christ's commandments, the more we are listening to his Spirit's call in our lives. And what are these commandments to which we have to listen? Jesus said the whole law and the prophets could be summarized as "You shall love the Lord your God with all your heart, and with all your soul, and with all your mind.... You shall love your neighbor as yourself" (Matt 22:37, 39). If this seems too general a statement, then Paul helps us fill out the details. Like Jesus, St. Paul tells us the law of love is not primarily revealed in what we say, or how we feel, but in what we do. Christian love is an intensely practical affair. When we are patient, kind, and gentle with each other, we are obeying the law of love. So too when we forgive each other, tell the truth, and remain faithful, we are listening most carefully to Christ's commandments.

32

Encountering God

Acts 1:12–14; 1 Peter 4:13–16; John 17:1–11a

In the Acts of the Apostles, we are told that the earliest church was constantly devoting themselves to prayer, and John's Gospel has Jesus praying for himself and his followers. One of the unexpected gifts of Easter is the ease with which we should be able to pray. Our God cannot do more to show us how real and powerful his love for us is than in the life, death, and resurrection of Jesus. Through Jesus, we have been brought into the family of God, and our prayer is like dinnertime conversation, catching up on how the day is going and alerting our father and brother to what's in store in the coming days.

We do not have to *do* anything in prayer. God does not need a show from us, in fact the more we pretend before God, the more God must wonder why we are going through this routine. We just have to be available to God and experience God's loving presence in any way that helps us draw closer to the one who created, loves, sustains, and saves us. What helps one person in prayer may not help someone else, and so the rich diversity in the church's tradition in prayer reflects the variety of ways we can encounter God. The best rule of thumb I know for prayer is: "if it helps, do it; if it doesn't, don't."

33

Go in Peace

Acts 1:1–11; Ephesians 1:17–23;
Matthew 28:16–20

Matthew tells us that the eleven men worshipped Jesus, who commissioned them to go out to the world and promised that he would stay with them until the end of time.

Worship is a word that Catholics don't often use. While other denominations describe their liturgy as "worship," we tend to use it only in a more secular way as in "hero worship" or "not an altar at which I worship." The concept behind this word, however, is an important one. To worship God is to admit that we are not God. We are creatures and our worship is directed toward our Creator, Savior, and Sustainer.

Whether we realize it or not, we are commissioned to go out to the world at the end of every liturgy: "Go in peace to love and serve the Lord." This changes our worship. We are not here just for ourselves. Mass, which comes from a word meaning "to be sent," indicates that our liturgy is about celebrating what God has done in the world in and through us, and is a preparation for what God still wants to accomplish.

Finally, we continue to experience the abiding presence of Christ in our daily lives or else we would not be here. God, as revealed in Jesus Christ, is not distant to our lives or impervious to our needs; we believe in a companion-God, who seeks our company as much as we need God's.

34

Peace and Forgiveness

Acts 2:1–11; 1 Corinthians 12:3b–7, 12–13; John 20:19–23

Sometimes we can think that peace and quiet is sitting in the lotus position in a darkened room. Christ's gift of peace is more robust than that. Peace is like all the best things in life: an attitude of mind and a habit born of consistently making good choices. Some people can do a large amount of work and be quite serene. Peace, for them, is an affair of the mind and a way of life.

If we really want to cultivate peace and quiet in our lives, we need to confront the things we are trying to avoid or deny. Often these things hinge on painful memories or events where we were destructive toward others, or they were toward us. Unless we forgive ourselves or forgive them, our busy-ness will ensure that we have enough clamor and activity to stay away from ugly memories. Unfortunately, it usually follows that, when we are so busy not dealing with the sins of our past, peace and quiet stay far away from us as well.

Let us pray that, while the Spirit might allow us to retain any sins, we choose Jesus's first option this Pentecost and forgive as generously as we can those who have tried to crucify us. We might have to forgive ourselves as well. And then, like Jesus, with old wounds exposed, we can rejoice that the Spirit has breathed into us the greatest gift of all: the peace and quiet we most crave and need.

ORDINARY TIME—II

35

Good Relationships

Exodus 34:4b–6, 8–9;
2 Corinthians 13:11–13;
John 3:16–18

The special insight into God that we celebrate today is that relationships are at the very center of who God is.

We believe that the God who creates, redeems, and sustains the world seeks us out and invites us into a loving relationship. This is what gives us our greatest dignity and urges us on to share this message with everyone we meet. What a privilege! What an invitation! What a God!

It also follows that if relationships are at the core of God, then, for those of us who accept the invitation into the Trinity's embrace, relationships are meant to be our core business too. We are not to be isolated believers or private disciples. The degree to which we understand the feast of the Trinity will be shown in the care we take in our many and varied relationships, be they social, intimate, professional, civic, or international.

Every time we do anything to form new and good relationships, mend those that are broken, help other relationships to be deeper and richer, or just enjoy the ones we have, we discover one thing: Trinity Sunday is a moveable feast.

36

Real Food and Drink

Deuteronomy 8:2–3, 14b–16a;
1 Corinthians 10:16–17;
John 6:51–58

When we receive the Risen Christ in communion, we do not say "Amen" to a symbol of his presence or a sign of his life. It is Christ who hosts us, who gives us himself so that we might be transformed into his image and likeness. In modern language, Christ says to us at every Mass, "Here I am, broken and poured out in love for you. Take me. I'm here for you."

The danger with all gifts, and most especially with this gift, is that we can think it's just for us, an intimate moment between each of us and Christ....Augustine taught that if we were not better people, working for unity and loving each other away from the Eucharist, it fails to achieve its purpose.

The God who comes to us at every Eucharist as real food is the same God who asks, "When I was hungry did you feed me?" This question says that just as God feeds us, so we too should and can feed each other.

37

Reverence

Deuteronomy 11:18, 26–28, 32;
Romans 3:21–25a, 28; Matthew 7:21–27

The Hebrew word for fear of the Lord is *yare*, and rather than meaning to be terrified of God, it is better translated as "reverence," which puts an altogether different complexion on what sort of believer the Bible is calling us to be.

A friend of mine once told me that such was the loving respect and admiration he had for his father, the most cutting thing his dad ever said to him was "I am disappointed in you." That comes close to helping us translate into our vernacular what fear of the Lord is all about.

When we admire and respect someone, we don't want to let them down; we want to emulate their achievements and grow in their esteem. Their love of us doesn't put us down, it builds us up, and it helps us love ourselves. It changes us for the better. This is what our reverence for God is all about.

If we have a genuine and real reverence for the Lord, if we have built our house of faith on rock, then we will never want to let God down, not because God will curse us if we do, but because we have been given the gifts at baptism to be "guts-and-glory believers."

And that is the will of the Father—that we be people of integrity who mean what we say and practice what we preach, at home and on the days when we are translated to other places where life takes us.

38

Here and Now

Hosea 6:3–6; Romans 4:18–25;
Matthew 9:9–13

What I like best about Ordinary Time is that it values the everyday, predictable routine that makes up most of our lives. If we had no Ordinary Time, we would not be able to celebrate extraordinary feasts; we would be at fever pitch all the time. This would be unsustainable and unhelpful. It would be a bit like celebrating birthdays every day. After a while, they would lose their shine. So, the church now asks us to settle into weeks of celebrating the quiet processes of our lives.

On the Sundays in Ordinary Time, we indicate that the Risen Christ can be found in moments we might think of as tedious, uneventful, and humdrum.

We can be so busy planning and looking for spectacular occasions we do not pay sufficient attention to the seemingly banal details of each day and to the relationships that form the foundations of our happiness.

The Gospel indicates that Jesus calls us as we are—sinners—and where we are—in the normal world in which we live. We can, if we really want to, start again and reconstruct a better life transformed by his love. Every day provides us with a choice to be converted by his love and live our ordinary lives to the full.

39

Compassion

Exodus 19:2–6a; Romans 5:6–11; Matthew 9:36—10:8

This week's readings are about compassion. The Lord claims the Israelites as his treasured possession out of compassion. St. Paul reminds us that God sent the Son to save us from our own destructiveness because God had compassion on us in our sinfulness. And when Jesus saw the crowds, he had compassion for their diseases, sufferings, and lack of leadership, and he did something about it.

We are called to see the crowds of our own day and be moved with compassion. Coming from the Latin words *co* meaning "with," and *pati* meaning "to suffer," compassion asks us to imagine what it's like to be a refugee, homeless, a victim of domestic violence, HIV positive, substance addicted, a person of color, or unemployed.

We may not be able to answer these people's suffering or perhaps for some reason we should not be the ones to respond to their suffering. In either event, what we should do is secondary to how we feel with them.

Jesus doesn't teach us today to solve all the world's problems, just that we have to have the right attitude toward our brothers and sisters, imagining what it's like for them and treating them in the way we would want to be treated....At that point, our understanding will be touching the Divine.

40

Taking the Risk

Jeremiah 20:10–13; Romans 5:12–15; Matthew 10:26–33

Today's Gospel reminds us that there is a middle road between denying what should be acknowledged and dealt with and being absorbed by it.

The church rightly holds that the best psychological tools can bring into the open memories and experiences that can be seen for what they are and dealt with. Long before the therapist's office, Christ enabled the church to develop the sacrament of penance, where we admit our most destructive behavior and hear that we are forgiven and healed. At that moment, the love of God is active in us drawing out what Christ wants in the light, spoken of, and healed.

Jesus invites all of us to find a person we respect and trust, and to end the tyranny of the power of secrets and lies. When we take this risk with the appropriate person, the presence of God won't be far away.

41

A Chrstian Response

2 Kings 4:8–11, 14–16a;
Romans 6:3–4, 8–11;
Matthew 10:37–42

These days, interdenominational marriages are rarely the reasons over which a family will divide. But we know that other religious issues can still break up a family. It's always a tragedy when this happens.

From today's Gospel, we know that the same family heartbreak occurred in the early church. At this time, however, Christianity was the small sect drawing believers away from Judaism, to acknowledge Jesus as the Messiah. They lost their old life and found a new one in Christ.

There can be moments when a family's lifestyle, beliefs, behavior, or values are such that one member feels that, in conscience, or by conviction, he or she does not belong anymore. When this happens, we can listen carefully to the reasons the family member gives. Maybe we *have* lost something essential in our life together that needs challenge and change. And maybe it's the family member who is in the wrong.

Keeping the lines of communication open, speaking the truth with calmness and love, and remaining as compassionate as possible are the best Christian responses.

42

Come to Me

Zechariah 9:9–10; Romans 8:9, 11–13; Matthew 11:25–30

Our faith is not about praying away our problems or fears and wishing it were otherwise. Our faith means we have experienced the love of God in Jesus Christ so that we never carry our burdens alone. God is our companion and guide, and, as with every Christian community, we are called to be the place wherein we carry each other's burdens and rest with each other awhile.

Jesus didn't come to us as a divine magician, waving a wand over our problems to wipe away all our tears. Rather, he accompanies us so he can show us that the gift of peace and a release from our life's burdens are often found in having the perspective to exercise the gift of right judgment. Making the best possible choices can lead to the alleviation of our pain and difficulties.

As we know, for some of our difficulties, there is no spiritual quick fix. There is no cheap grace. The answer is not simply Jesus. In confronting issues, however, it is necessary for spiritual and mental health to take time out, to be as gentle with ourselves as possible, and to know that the burden of life is best shared with others.

43

Sowers and Reapers

Isaiah 55:10–11; Romans 8:18–23; Matthew 13:1–23

In recent years the church has regularly reminded us that the issue of caring for the environment is an important part of our Christian commitment for justice, part of the seamless garment in our ethic of life. We have been reminded that while the earth has been entrusted to us as stewards to be preserved, it is also given into our hands to be developed in such a way that there will be a productive earth for future generations to inherit.

If this means we must limit our consumption, change our priorities regarding energy and trade, and develop eco-friendly industries, then all the better for us. Most of us know that we cannot keep going as we are, with ever increasing unsustainable demands on our planet.

The Old and New Testaments are filled with the importance of our relationships to the earth. In the Book of Genesis humanity is told to care for and subdue the earth, not wreck it. We cannot be irresponsible about the world's finite resources in the hope that we will find solutions in the future. Avarice is not one of the seven deadly sins for nothing.

We believe the bread and wine of the Eucharist, which we say are "the fruit of the earth and the work of human hands," are changed into Christ present among us. May these eucharistic gifts rooted in our soil effect in us a change that might enable us to have ears to hear the groan of creation as it calls for us to be more careful sowers and responsible reapers.

44

The Word of God

Wisdom 12:13, 16–19; Romans 8:26–27;
Matthew 13:24–43

To be a Christian is to ponder the word of God. That's why the Second Vatican Council encouraged us all to return to regular private reflection on the Bible. Along with this encouragement the council also reminded us, however, that as strong as the feelings and revelations we experience in our private scriptural prayer may be, these may have little or no consequence for the wider community of faith. We believe that the whole church has the task to discern where the word of God is leading us.

To help this discernment, our scholars, who pay great attention to the history and the literary, textual, and cultural issues in and around the Bible, have always aided the Catholic community. We place great weight on the "here and now" of the faith community who listens to the word of God and lives it out.

We hold, however, that the scriptures are not books of facts, though they contain historical information. The word of God is for us the pathway to faith, a series of revealed and inspired portraits of God and a distillation of God's saving love for us and our response.

When there are inconsistencies or differences, rather than unsettle us, we see them as examples of the various rich approaches to the truth of our salvation in and through Christ.

45

Heaven and Hell

1 Kings 3:5, 7–12; Romans 8:28–30;
Matthew 13:44–52

Old-time missioners used to have a field day with today's Gospel, or at least with part of it. While they may have liked the passages that suggested that heaven was *like* a treasure in a field or *like* a pearl of great price, they told us that hell *was* a furnace of fire where there was weeping and gnashing of teeth.

There are two major differences, however, between how we used to speak about heaven and hell and what we say now. Just as we know the treasure hidden in the field or the pearl of great price are metaphors for heaven, rich and wonderful ones at that, they remain images that enable us to grasp an unimaginable concept. So it is with hell. How can we imagine life without love and God? All we can confidently say is that hell is non-God.

The second change is that we are more careful about being so confident regarding who is going there. Jesus tells us that God wants all humanity to be saved. We can't take that seriously and then have people slip into hell for a small infringement of the rules.

Humanity can also be seen as the treasure in the field that God has sold everything to own. We are the pearl of great price that God has moved heaven and earth to possess, and we are the fish caught up in the net of God's love.

46

Abundance

Isaiah 55:1–3; Romans 8:35, 37–39;
Matthew 14:13–21

The church has always believed that the feeding of the crowd prefigured the Eucharist, this weekly time where we receive the fullness of God's word, through the life of the community, the minister, and the transformation of the bread and wine.

It's all about abundance. Our God has abundantly provided for us so that we can abundantly provide for the entire world that is given into our care. "From everyone to whom much has been given, much will be required; and from the one to whom much has been entrusted, even more will be demanded" (Luke 12:48). The problem is that when we look around, we see that while some of us have so much, others have nothing at all.

If this reality doesn't move us to a change of heart and right action, then we have not understood the story of the loaves and the fish, that God's goodness is never intended for a select few.

Sometimes people look at the poverty in the world and think, "How could God allow that?" This question can cause us to feel distant from God, but given all God has given us and our ability to share from the abundance we have, the right question to ask is "Guess who's moved away from whom?"

47

The Son of God

1 Kings 19:9a, 11–13a; Romans 9:1–5; Matthew 14:22–33

Poor old Job found God amid a storm, and winds and waves are a common Old Testament shorthand for the perils of life. The image of the boat was an early symbol for the church, and Matthew has all Jesus's disciples in it. Jesus hovering over the waters has echoes of the action of the Spirit in the first account of creation in Genesis. Even Jesus restoring calm to the sea follows from what the prophet Jonah had done before.

Matthew's account is magnificent on its own terms, but with these details we can begin to see his theological message. Jesus, the Son of God and Lord of creation, remains faithful to the disciples, no matter how treacherous the seas or how great their fear. He comes to them so that they may be saved and re-created as the church who recognizes that he is the fulfillment of creation, the one whom Israel has been longing to see and embrace.

We are inheritors of Matthew's faith. We're here because we believe that Jesus is the Son of God who has saved us from ourselves and from destruction. But it also means that in every storm that threatens our lifeboat Jesus comes to call us to faith, to catch us when we think we're drowning, to accompany us back to safety, and to bring calm to the troubled seas of our life.

48

Courage and Persistence

Isaiah 56:1, 6–7; Romans 11:13–15, 29–32; Matthew 15:21–28

Until quite recently in many cultures around the world, events or experiences that had no ready explanation were put down to evil forces. This was certainly true in Jesus's day.

The Syro-Phoenician woman considers herself cursed for having a daughter who is tormented by a demon. It is very unlikely that her daughter is possessed by the devil. She probably had a chronic illness that could not be cured. Furthermore, the woman is also considered cursed by others because she is a Gentile.

Because of her ethnicity and religion, the disciples do not think she should ask for anything from Jesus. He seems to concur with them. If it wasn't for the woman's courage and persistence, she would never have got what she wanted. And by Jesus referring to them as dogs, he seems to agree with the contempt with which the Jews held the Gentiles.

It is the woman's quick wit and faith that turn the situation around. She argues that, if she is to be considered a dog, she is not a wild one but of the house variety where she should be able to enjoy the leftovers. The power of her insight and the rightness of her cause catch Jesus off guard, her daughter is healed, and everyone is taught a lesson about how the kingdom of God breaks through in the most extraordinary ways.

49

Who Is Jesus?

Isaiah 22:19–23; Romans 11:33–36;
Matthew 16:13–20

"Who do you say that I am?"

The disciples, reflecting on their experiences with Jesus, offer various possibilities, but it is Peter who says that Jesus is the revelation of God for the world. This is the great profession of faith and the basis on which the church comes into being.

And what was true then is true now. At some point, if we want our faith to move from being a code of law, a concept, or some excellent ideas, toward something we can experience, we must take the faith of the church, which has nurtured us up to now, and make it our own. In doing so, when we encounter Christ, we contribute to the refounding of the church in our generation.

Just being part of the "Catholic crowd" is hardly the challenge Jesus presents to the disciples in today's Gospel. We are commissioned like the disciples to bear witness to Christ's personal love in the workplace, with our friends, and in our families.

And it all hinges on that great question that is asked of each of us today: "Who do you say that I am?" How we answer this question reveals so much, including whether Christ is an idea we like or the object of our passion.

50

Suffering

Jeremiah 20:7–9; Romans 12:1–2;
Matthew 16:21–27

Christians are not meant to be smiling masochists. We are not meant to be lovers of pain—just bearers of it.

We are invited, by Jesus, to see the burden of suffering in our lives as an opportunity to be faithful to his example. It also gives us an opportunity to be in solidarity with all those who suffer in our world. This is easier said than done. When we suffer in our daily lives, thoughts of others rarely come to mind easily, but it can be consoling to keep our suffering in context and know that we are not facing it alone.

Today's Gospel shows the edge involved in being a follower of Christ. I don't know of a more demanding vocation in our world than that of taking up the cross of being faithful, loving, and selfless.

If we have the eyes to see it and the humility to accept it, Christ, literally, hangs in there with us every step of the way. So, let's recall the first cross from which we take comfort as we bear our own crosses, "In the name of the Father, the Son, and the Holy Spirit. Amen."

51

Self-Esteem

Ezekiel 33:7–9; Romans 13:8–10;
Matthew 18:15–20

For St. Paul, love of self was not indulgent, but the cornerstone of our mission to love as Jesus loves us. Paul knew the difference between self-love and self-adoration. Our love of God is expressed in the healthy and appropriate esteem we have for ourselves. Put another way, we cannot love anyone else if we don't love ourselves. If we have poor self-esteem, then we often need others to fill up this gap in our self-love. Most relationships cannot sustain such a demand.

Jesus in today's Gospel attends to this destructive side of our human nature. Jesus teaches us that those who do not love their neighbor as they should are to be treated with dignity and respect and offered every opportunity to seek forgiveness until it is clear they can no longer be a part of the Christian family.

The challenge and hallmark of the Christian life is the way in which we live out God's love and forgiveness....The love and forgiveness of God does not mean that "anything goes." It is a love that calls for constant conversion. We can witness to it only to the degree that we have experienced it, from God, from others, and in the way we love and forgive ourselves.

52

The Heart of God

Sirach 27:30—28:7; Romans 14:7–9; Matthew 18:21–35

In the fifth century, St. Augustine said that forgiveness was like a mother who has two wonderful daughters named Justice and Compassion. In using such a metaphor Augustine knew that forgiveness was not a one-time event; it was a process that involved other virtues as well. Jesus teaches a similar lesson in today's Gospel, where he uses the image of the king settling his debts. Because the king is just, compassionate, and forgiving, he rightly expects that, in turn, his steward will be so as well.

It's easy to be forgiving in the big picture. We can talk strongly about war, peace, and reconciliation. It's quite another to forgive those closest to us. Sometimes the hardest place to be compassionate and just is in our own home. If we are not speaking with a husband, wife, child, parent, sibling, friend, or member of our community, then today's Gospel has a strong challenge right where we live.

Jesus doesn't tell us that forgiveness is easy, just necessary. To forgive someone in our family, workplace, our circle of friends, or in our church is not to pretend that a sinful situation did not occur, but to face it head-on and demand justice with compassion.

When we choose forgiveness over revenge, and love over hate, we begin to glimpse God's creative goodness coming to perfection in us, because forgiveness is a participation in the very heart of God.

53

God's Greatness

Isaiah 55:6–9; Philippians 1:20c–24, 27a; Matthew 20:1–16a

In today's Gospel, in which the first laborers are paid the same wage as the afternoon workers, what the early birds didn't reckon on was that they could have come much later and got the same deal....This wasn't how it was supposed to be!

This story, then, is a wonderful commentary on how fickle we are and, luckily for us, how extraordinarily generous God is. What we see in ourselves and others is only a glimpse of what God is like. God is so much more: more loving, more forgiving, more compassionate, and more just.

And because God is so much greater than anything we could ask or imagine, we are constantly surprised at how he overturns our expectations. We look for God in the big and spectacular and he comes to us poor, naked, sick, in prison, and hungry. God speaks through the most surprising people at the most surprising times.

Rather than being resentful, let's thank God for being bigger than we are and for being just to all of us, no matter when, or how, we get the word.

54

The Least

Ezekiel 18:25–28; Philippians 2:1–11;
Matthew 21:28–32

"Truly I tell you, the tax collectors and the prostitutes are going into the kingdom of god ahead of you."

It's hard for us to imagine what a diverse and scandalous group in many respects the first fathers and mothers of our faith were seen to be. Imagine, if you will, the fuss that would still be created if the local bishop was seen constantly dining with women in prostitution, drug dealers, or known terrorists. People would be outraged, but the bishop would be doing nothing short of following Jesus's example. This situation gives us a little insight into how affronted the Chief Priests and Pharisees were by Jesus and, in turn, by his disciples' behavior.

For Jesus there was never a lost case, or a person beyond help. He didn't just spend time with the poor and broken of his society, but offered them a new way of life, an opportunity to start again, and redemption from their destructive behavior....We constantly look for Christ in the spectacular and the wonderful and he comes to us in the least of our brothers and sisters.

55

"Ah-ha" Moments

Isaiah 5:1–7; Philippians 4:6–9; Matthew 21:33–43

There are often facets of our personality or character that we are ashamed of or about which we despair. From gossip to greed, past hurts to anger, sexuality to broken relationships, we can often get discouraged at how un-together our Christian life is.

Even though we have worked hard to overcome our worst traits, we often think nothing good will ever come of them. In such a context we need to hear today's Gospel, "The stone that the builders rejected has become the cornerstone; this was the Lord's doing, and it is amazing in our eyes."

The parts of our character we most despise could be the most marvelous moments of amazing grace. Nothing is irredeemable to God; nothing has gone too far or become too entrenched. In the Christian life there is no room for shame, only for repentance and starting over. Looking at things we have thought of as only being problems provides us with the greatest potential for "ah-ha" moments, where the healing and love of Christ enable us to turn our lives around, to demolish all the negative and defeatist self-talk in which we can indulge and rebuild ourselves with Christ, the master builder.

It's amazing how many "ah-ha" moments we have as our history ceases to be a problem to be overcome and becomes a challenge to be harnessed for building the kingdom of God on earth.

56

The Invitation

Isaiah 25:6–10a; Philippians 4:12–14, 19–20; Matthew 22:1–14

In the parable of the king's banquet, Jesus foreshadows the days when those whom one would expect to be Christian would reject the invitation to faith, and when those thought least likely to respond to God's call would flock into the church.

Since the earliest days of Christianity, the wedding banquet was seen as a metaphor for two things: the Eucharist and eternal life. Curiously, this parable, while using the imagery of the banquet, is less concerned about the meal and more about who's in and who's out, and why!

We can see this through the tenants who turn down the opportunity to go to a royal wedding or a presidential reception—still an almost unimaginable thing to do. It's seen in the poor who recognize the gift and the giver, get dressed up, and have somewhere to go. And it's seen in the impostor who is not correctly dressed for the occasion and is speechless when called to account.

So, what does all this have to say to us? It's not about how one dresses for Mass or for eternal life! It is about being poor enough to recognize the gift of God in the invitation to faith and about being generous enough to respond completely. For taking care about what we say and do, the values by which we live our lives at home, at work, at play, and in the way we relate to each other is how we show that we mean what we profess.

57

Church and State

Isaiah 45:1, 4–6; 1 Thessalonians 1:1–5b; Matthew 22:15–21

Christian leaders, who are charged to proclaim and defend the gospel, are obliged to use whatever forum necessary to declare that God's personal love encompasses everyone and everything under heaven. As the prophet Isaiah reminds us, God calls each one of us by name.

At times we may not agree with our religious leaders; we may think them ill informed; we may even think they have overstepped the mark. If this is the case we should write to them, encourage them to consider other perspectives and to broaden the basis upon which they make their judgments. But we should never be seduced by those who want the church sidelined from the mainstream of the debates that shape the way we live, the values we share, the laws we draft, and the priorities we draw up for our human community.

If the church shows disinterest in any of this, it is untrue to the very things for which Jesus lived, died, and was raised from the dead. We should give to Caesar all that Caesar is justly entitled to have for the sake of the common good. A higher allegiance, however, goes to God, who will call all Caesars to account for what they have done and what they failed to do. And we might be asked to explain how we let them get away with it in the first place.

58

Hospitality

Exodus 22:20–26; 1 Thessalonians 1:5c–10;
Matthew 22:34–40

In Exodus, the Lord tells us today, "You shall not wrong or oppress a resident alien, for you were aliens in the land of Egypt." Jesus tells us in the Gospel that the love of God is fulfilled precisely when we love our neighbor.

In today's Gospel, Jesus does not promise us that the love of God and neighbor is going to cost us nothing. Jesus's law of love involves sacrifice for us individually and as a nation. Through the acceptance of this teaching, we are committing ourselves to being our neighbor's keeper. Sadly, many of us want a good life for ourselves, while doing very little to help other countries become more livable, and then we can reject people who want to share in the blessings we have worked for and inherited.

The Gospel of Matthew gives us the story of Mary, Joseph, and Jesus being forced to flee Israel for Egypt as refugees. If the Holy Family was coming our way these days, they might be sent back to King Herod. May our goodness and hospitality mirror on earth the welcome we hope to enjoy from Jesus, Mary, and Joseph in the kingdom that is promised to all, irrespective of where any of us has been born.

59

Hypocrisy

Malachi 1:14b—2:2b, 8–10;
1 Thessalonians 2:7b—9:13; Matthew 23:1–12

Today's Gospel sums up what it's been like for many of us to hear about how some priests betrayed our trust, how many victims were disbelieved, and how a few of our bishops have tried to cover up criminal actions. We have seen the exalted being humbled and the humble being exalted.

Jesus tells the crowds to listen to what the Pharisees teach, but not to follow their appalling example. The behavior of the Pharisees has a name, hypocrisy, and it's one of the reasons we have received such a public pasting in recent times. Some of it has been justified. We have been seen to be a community more interested in our good name and public standing than in the damage done to those brothers and sisters of ours who were given into our care and became victims of physical and sexual abuse. We have been exposed as not practicing what we preach.

If we are going to be faithful to all of Jesus's teaching and the entire Christian tradition, then we must comfort and heal the victims of abuse and call the perpetrators to the demands of the law, treatment, and reconciliation. But we also believe that the only way to healing is through forgiveness. True forgiveness never runs from the truth or minimizes our sinfulness. It confronts the human condition with justice and compassion for all concerned.

60

Living the Present

Wisdom 6:12–16; 1 Thessalonians 4:13–18; Matthew 25:1–13

Think of the times when we are going to have a difficult interview or a conversation we would rather not have. We play out in our mind how the interaction will run. It rarely goes how we imagine, and often our anxiety and fear have been misplaced. What is curious is that on the next occasion we go through the same process of trying to live the future all over again.

The early church thought Jesus would return quickly. There was a crisis of faith when he didn't. Some Christians lived as though this imminent return was a fact. We are still waiting. Matthew tells us, then, that the Christian life is about wisdom, right judgment, and reading the signs of the times.

St. Ignatius tells us the best way to prepare for the future is to let go of the unhealed past, as best as we can, and live in the here and now. The Holy Spirit helps us see what needs to be done today and what preparation is necessary for tomorrow. This is such simple and sound advice and yet many of us don't follow it. It takes nothing for us to feel the hurt and pain of our past or to be consumed by the future.

Alcoholics Anonymous sums it up neatly when it tells us to take life "one day at a time," which is another way of saying what Matthew's community came to see, "Keep awake, therefore, for you know neither the day nor the hour."

61

Our Gifts

Proverbs 31:10–13, 19–20, 30–31;
1 Thessalonians 5:1–6; Matthew 25:14–30

It is almost possible that Jesus had women in mind when he shared the parable of the talents in today's Gospel. What can often get lost in the debates about who should be ordained in today's church is that women have always and still "lead" the church in powerful and long-lasting ways. From the extraordinary abilities of religious and lay women in Catholic welfare, education, health care, overseas missions, and theological institutions to wives and mothers who daily witness to the fidelity and goodness of God, this all reveals in innumerable ways the power of the parable of the talents. The reality is that if it were not for women's leadership, commitment, and faith, it would be difficult to see how the church and our ministries could survive.

None of this minimizes the pain and hurt some women have experienced at the hands of the church. Some feel as though their specific contribution to the life of the church has not been fully realized.

All we can hope and pray for is that we may find ways to use everyone's talents for the building up of the kingdom of God, and that we may see that everyone's contribution, irrespective of gender, is precious and worthy of praise.

62

Christ the King

Ezekiel 34:11–12, 15–17;
1 Corinthians 15:20–26, 28; Matthew 25:31–46

The Roman emperor Constantine was baptized in 337. In 313, a few years before his death, Constantine had already declared that Christianity was to be the new state religion.

It cannot surprise us that after Constantine's conversion the image of Christ the King becomes one of the most popular ones used in religious art. Up to this time the image of Jesus as the Good Shepherd was the most represented. After 313, however, Jesus is dressed in royal robes, with a crown, scepter, and orb. Mary is often presented in similar dress and starts to be called the Queen of Heaven.

The problem with all this is not that worldly imperial language was now being used in reference to Jesus. He described himself as a king. Christianity started to forget that Jesus also pointed out that his kingdom was "not of this world" and that his courtiers could be recognized by how they feed the hungry, water the thirsty, welcome strangers, clothe the naked, care for the sick, and visit prisoners—an altogether different order from that usually prized in worldly kingdoms.

On the last day of the church's year, we are challenged by Christ our King to give our true allegiance to what really matters. Not ambition, greed, status, and power, but the quiet revolutionary work of making the world a more just and peaceful place for everyone to live in. To the degree that we do this we are witnesses to the real meaning of Christ's reign in our lives.

www.ingramcontent.com/pod-product-compliance
Lightning Source LLC
LaVergne TN
LVHW020652100826
845148LV00012B/2456

9780809149704